MOLLI

THE MAD BASHER

Malcolm Yorke

with illustrations by Margaret Chamberlain

DORLING KINDERSLEY
LONDON • NEW YORK • STUTTGART

A DORLING KINDERSLEY BOOK

First published in Great Britain in 1994
by Dorling Kindersley Limited,
9 Henrietta Street, London WC2E 8PS

Reprinted 1994, 1997

A CIP catalogue record for this book is
available from the British Library

ISBN 0-7513-7016-9

Colour reproduction by DOT Gradations Ltd.
Printed in Singapore

Molly Cuddle is a teacher. Her pupils like her very much because she reads them some great stories, they do lots of splashy painting, sing songs together, play recorders, and learn how things work.

3

Their classroom is always full of flowers
and interesting things to smell or taste
or fiddle about with and take to pieces.

Nobody in Molly Cuddle's class
is ever bored.

One Monday the class decided to do a project about the new shopping centre. You know the sort of thing. First, they read the centre's advertisements in the local paper. Next, Emma's group looked up the addresses in the phone book and wrote letters to the shopkeepers asking if the class could come and visit them.

Then Ali's group worked out the best way to get there on the map, and Derek and Mai's group made a list of questions to ask their families and neighbours about the shops they used. They were very busy all day.

"You've all worked very hard," said Molly Cuddle. "Now be careful on the way home, and I'll see you in the morning."

Molly Cuddle went home rather tired, but very pleased with her class. She had a pot of tea and some scones while she watched television. Then she fed her old cat, Cuddlebum. At seven o'clock she packed a bag, got into her little car, and drove off to the nearby city.

She parked near the Sports Stadium and went round the back to the Ladies' Changing Rooms. There she hung up her teaching clothes, took off her glasses, and put on a red costume. Then she pulled on a pair of long, red boots.

Finally she put red face paint over most of her face and drew on some terrible black eyebrows. She also wore a wild red wig. Across the back of her red costume was printed in big letters: MOLLY THE MAD BASHER.

Out she went into the stadium where a huge crowd booed and booed as she climbed through the ropes of a wrestling ring.

When her opponent, Pretty Polly, appeared on the opposite side of the stadium, the crowd began to cheer wildly, blow kisses, and sing.

FOR SHE'S A JOLLY GOOD LAY – YAY – DEE, AND SO SAY ALL OF US!

The announcer boomed into his microphone: "Laydeees and gennulmen. Tonight's contest is between …

"Your referee, laydeees and gennulmen, is Mike Thickear," said the announcer, and climbed out of the ring.

13

Clang! Round one!

Pretty Polly began by trying a half nelson, but the Basher wriggled free. She got Pretty Polly in a knee-press, then an aeroplane spin, and finally threw her right out of the ring into the second row of seats!

OOOAAAHH!

OWOWOW!

Round one to Molly the Mad Basher.

The crowd booed and booed.

14

Clang! Round two!

Pretty Polly drop-kicked the Basher, bounced her off the corner post, and sat on her head. The Basher bit Polly's bottom when the referee wasn't looking. But then Polly clinched it with a great body-slam on the Basher.

EEEEAAAOOoo!

THUD!

Round two to Pretty Polly.

The crowd loved it and cheered and cheered.

CHOKE

Clang! Round three!

Polly put the Basher in a full
nelson lock and tried to screw
her head right off her neck,
but the Basher got her back
with a pile-driver.

OOOOF!

Round three to Molly the Mad Basher.

"Cheat! Rotten! Get her off! Boooooo!"
howled the crowd.

16

Clang! Round four!

CRACK

BAM

They both leapt in feet first from their corners … and missed! The Basher's fist accidentally caught Mike Thickear on the jaw and he took a long time to recover. Then Polly got the Basher in a quick scissors, a flying mare, and a leg-stretch.

Round four to Pretty Polly.

The crowd whooped and whistled!

Clang! Clang! Round five!

Polly and the Basher tried everything they knew: fore arm smashes, strangle-holds, wrist locks, throttles, and even head butts. Neither gave way. Then in the last few seconds, the Basher tied Pretty Polly up in the ropes so she couldn't move and had to submit.

Molly the Mad Basher had won!

The crowd booed her all the way back
to the dressing-rooms.

Pretty Polly had to be carried back to the dressing-rooms on a stretcher, but the crowd clapped and cheered her all the way.

Molly the Mad Basher took off her face paint, her terrible eyebrows and wig, and became Molly Cuddle again. She showered, then nipped round to the corner café for a cup of coffee and a piece of cake with her best friend Dora.

It was Pretty Polly! Her real name was Dora Stibbs and she had only pretended to need a stretcher at the end of the bout. During the day Dora worked in a beauty parlour.

"I did like your pile-driver in the third round, dear," said Dora.

"Well, thank you Dora. And that was a lovely throttle you did in the last round – you must show me how you hold your fingers for that."

"I'd be glad to, Molly, but now I've got to dash for the baby-sitter. I do like to get back in time for the children's bedtime story."

"'Bye then, Dora. Your turn to win next week!" said Molly.

"'Bye Molly, thanks for the fun," said Dora, and away she went.

Molly Cuddle drove home. She ate a late supper, prepared her lessons for the next day, and went to bed tired and happy.

"Oh I **do** like Mondays," she said to Cuddlebum as she switched off the light.

On Tuesday and Wednesday, the class continued to prepare for their visit to the shopping centre. Emma's group made a plan of the centre, ready to fill in the names of the shops. Mai's and Ali's groups made lists of questions to ask the shoppers and shopkeepers. "Are there enough litter bins, and toilets, and fire exits? Can you get round in a wheelchair? What about seats for elderly people?"

They were all very busy and excited, including, of course, Molly Cuddle.

On Thursday, after assembly, the class followed Molly Cuddle in an orderly line to the shopping centre, chatting away as they went.

"Now, here we are. Notebooks and maps ready? Good," said Molly. "I think we'll begin with the jeweller's shop. Mr MacSparkle is expecting us and we're exactly on ..."

At that very moment there was a scream, a shout, and a crash! Two big men burst out of the jeweller's shop, stuffing trays of rings and watches into bags as they ran. They knocked over several of the children and pushed an elderly lady roughly aside.

But when the first one tried to push Molly Cuddle aside she gave him a punch on the jaw. Then she tossed the second one over her shoulder, did a scissors on the first, threw the second into the fountain, and slammed the first head down into a litter bin.

Then she fished them out and knotted their arms and legs together so tightly that they couldn't move a muscle. Mr MacSparkle called the police.

Molly wasn't even out of breath – though she did have a ladder in her tights!

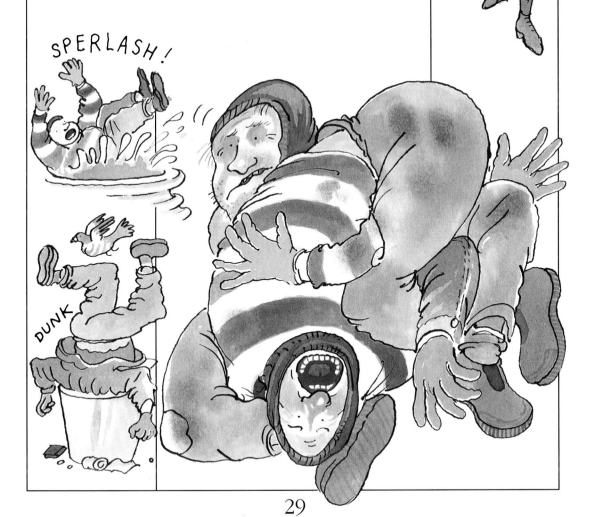

SPERLASH!

DUNK

The police arrived and bundled the robbers into their van. The crowds of shoppers and all the children booed and booed.

When Mr MacSparkle rushed up to
thank Miss Molly Cuddle, everyone
began to cheer and sing.

FOR SHE'S A JOLLY GOOD
LAY-YAY-DEE,
AND SO SAY
ALL OF US !

AMAZING!

DID YOU
SEE
THAT?

WONDERFUL !

31

"Wow! That was better than the wrestling on TV," said one of the crowd.

"Can we help you with your project?" asked an elderly lady.

"First, let's all give three cheers for Miss Molly Cuddle: Hip-hip-hooray!"

"Well," thought Molly. "It **is** nice not to be booed for once!"